Activity Book

1 Join the **m** things to Marshmallow Mouse.

2 Hop over to the **m** food.

Marshmallow Mouse

3 Give each mouse some milk.

Mice on a mat

4 Trace.

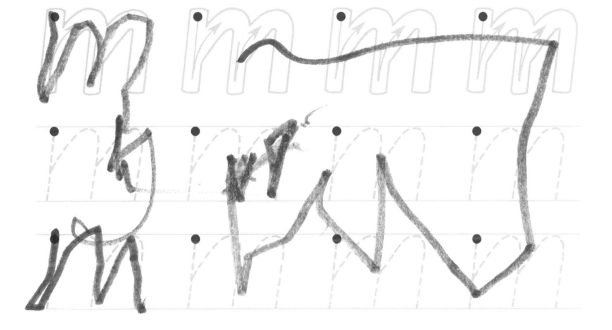

1 Join the **s** things to Sunny Snail.

2 Swirl down to the **s** food.

Sunny Snail

ABC
Reading
eggs

3 Give each snowman a smile.

Snowmen
with scarves

4 Trace.

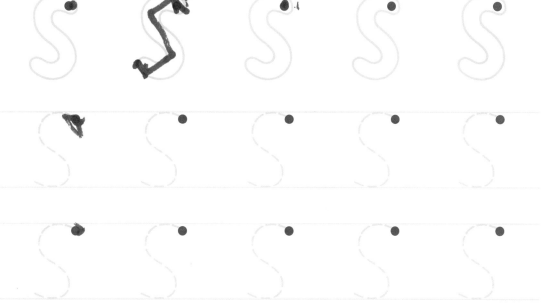

Lesson 3

1 Join the **i** things to Insillysect.

2 Join the **am** things to Pram Lamb.

3 Draw more insects on the igloo.

Insects on an igloo

4 Trace.

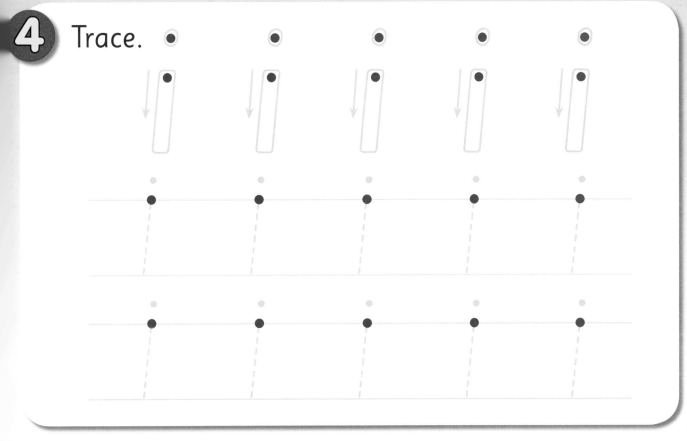

1 Complete the dot-to-dots.

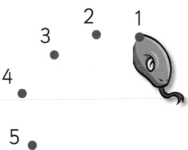

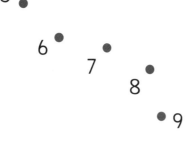
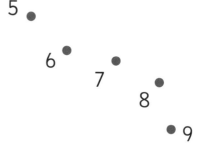

2 all the **m** .

m	m	m	m	m	m	m	j
m	t	i	m	z	x	m	k
m	s	u	m	b	g	m	h
m	q	o	m	f	c	m	n
m	r	p	m	n	a	m	d
m	w	n	m	r	w	m	v

8

③ **am** red, **m** blue, **s** green and **i** yellow.

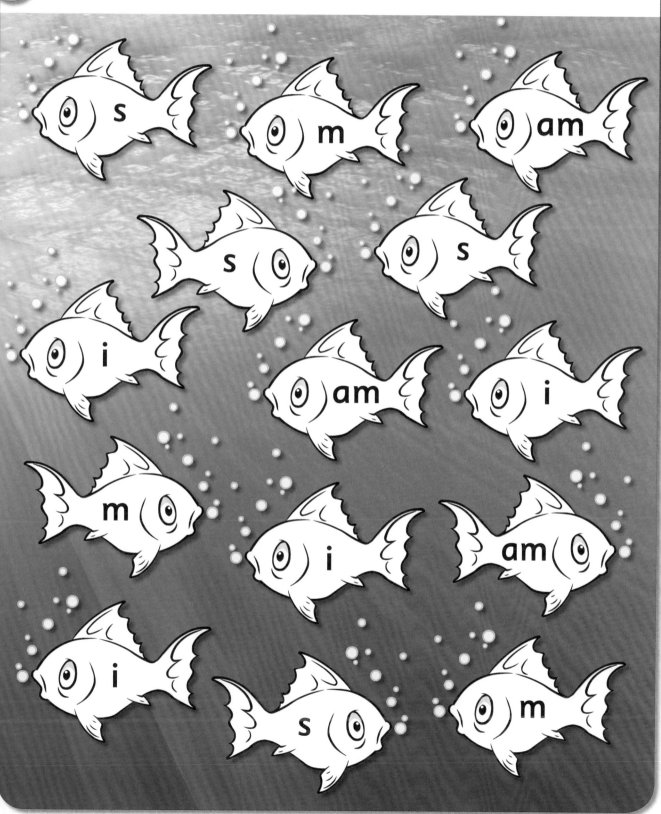

1 Join the **t** things to Tiger Turtle.

2 Finish Tiger Turtle's flowers.

Tiger Turtle

3 Give each teddy bear a toothbrush.

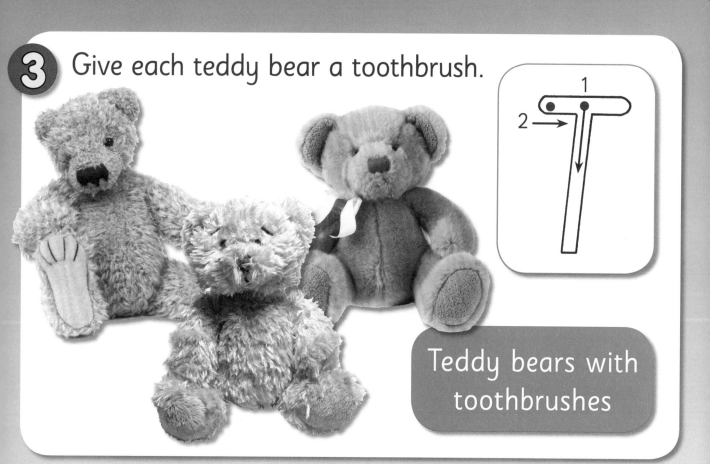

Teddy bears with toothbrushes

4 Trace.

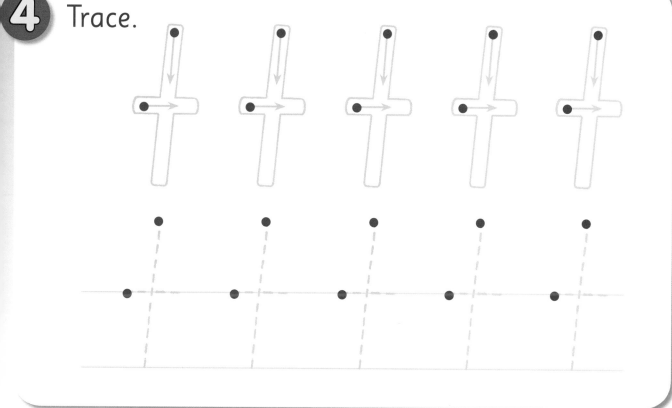

Lesson 5

1 Join the **a** things to Appley Ant.

2 Join the **at** things to Ding Bat.

3 Join the word to the picture.

cat

bat

rat

hat

4 Trace.

1 Complete the dot-to-dot.

5 •   9 •

1 •

4 •   8 •

6 •

2 •   10 •

3 •   7 •   11 •

2  all the **s** .

q	r	s	s	s	s	s	t	g
w	c	s	a	m	a	r	l	s
x	d	s	e	b	f	i	j	h
b	v	s	s	s	s	s	o	t
c	m	u	h	l	k	s	n	y
i	e	d	p	a	z	s	a	g
j	h	s	s	s	s	s	f	k

14

3 Join the critter to their food.

1 Join the **b** things to Beebee Bear.

2 Bounce over to the **b** food.

Beebee Bear

3 Draw a ball next to each bat.

Bats and balls

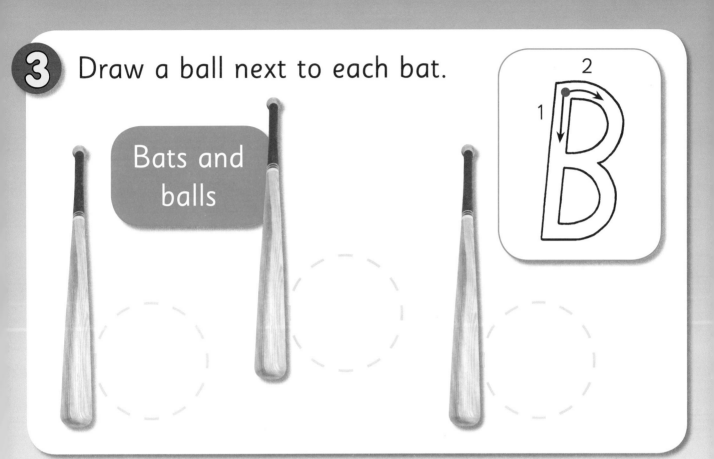

4 Trace.

1 Join the **c** things to Catty Cake.

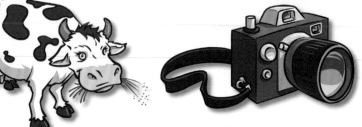

2 Add curls to the curly cat.

Catty Cake

3 Draw a caterpillar on each carrot.

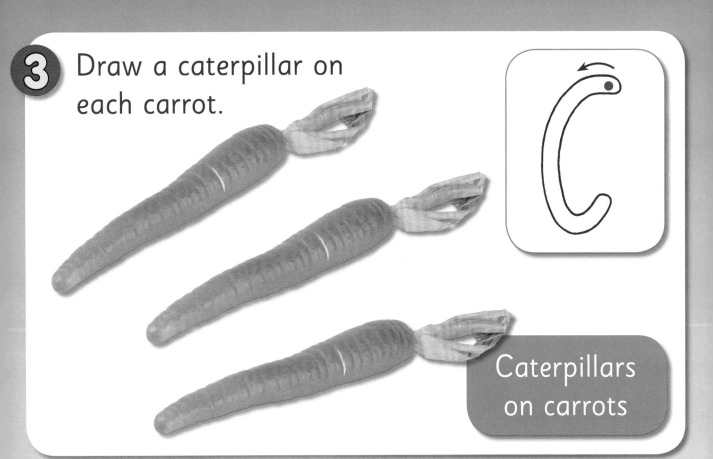

Caterpillars on carrots

4 Trace.

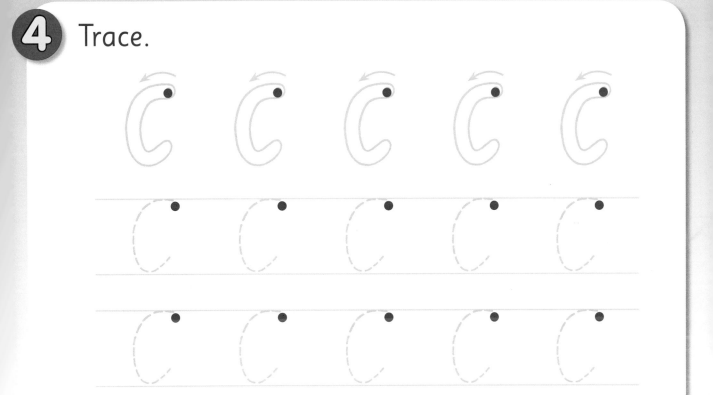

1 Join the **f** things to Frogfish.

2 Finish the flowers.

Frogfish

3 Join each fly to a fish.

Four fish eating flies

4 Trace.

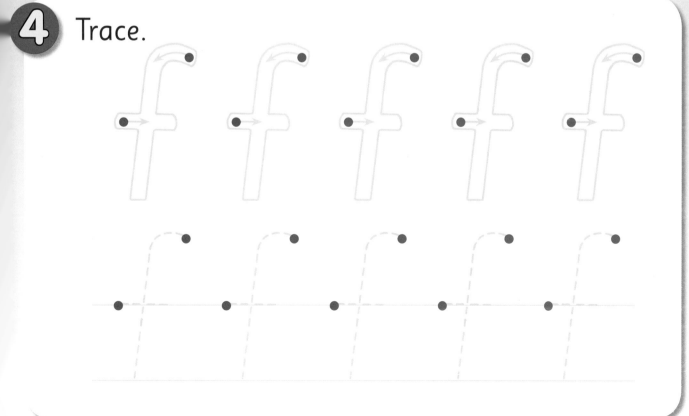

1 Complete the dot-to-dot.
Which letter did you make?

2 •
1 •

3 •

4 •

5 •   6 •

b

c

t

2 all the **b** .

p	a	i	b	t	c	d	g	o
o	t	s	b	k	e	f	r	j
t	s	n	b	a	l	n	k	r
r	p	w	b	b	b	b	z	k
q	j	m	b	l	d	b	e	s
d	x	v	b	a	m	b	n	m
e	u	i	b	b	b	b	h	t

3 Make words. Join to a picture.

c a

h a

s a

b a

m a

1 I red and **am** green.

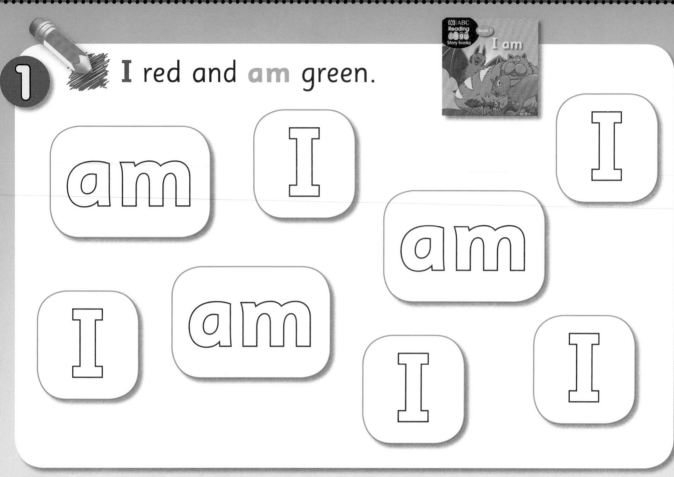

2 Join the word to the picture.

Sam

bat

cat

fat

3 Read each sentence. Join to a picture.

I am a cat.

I am a bat.

I am a fat cat.

I am Sam.

1 Finish each word.

2 Write each word. Read.

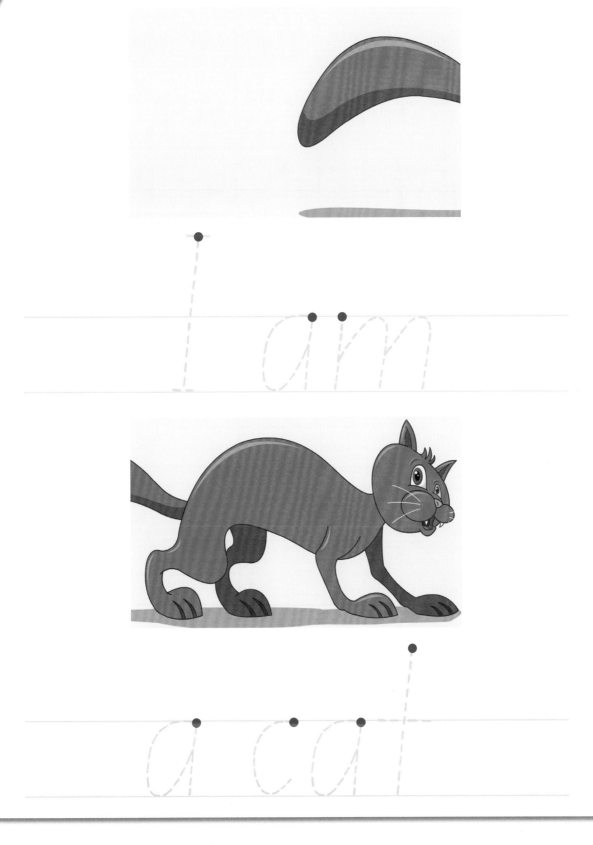

ian

a cat

Fun spot 4

1 **f** red and **t** blue.

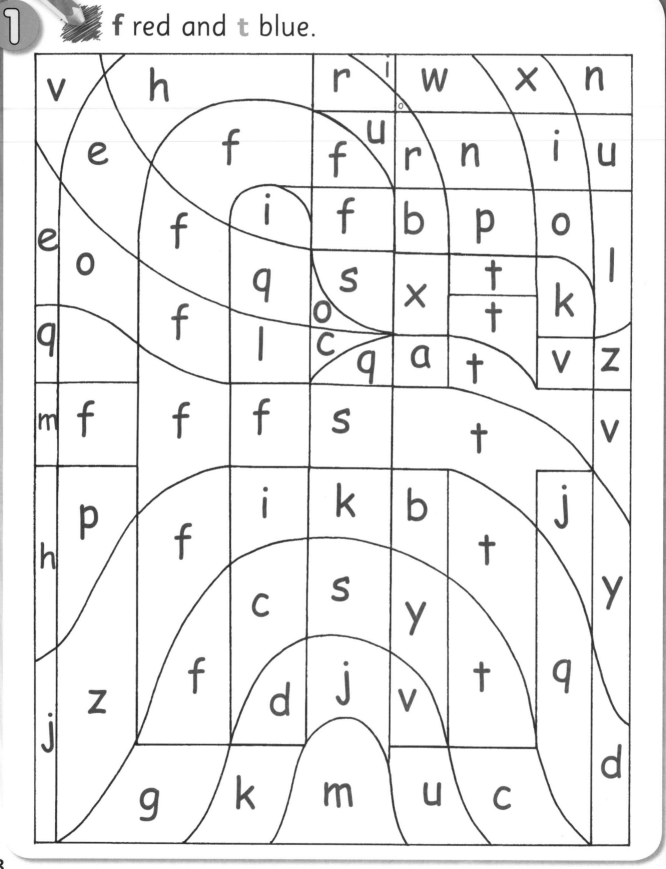

28

2 Join the critter to their food.

1 Trace and .

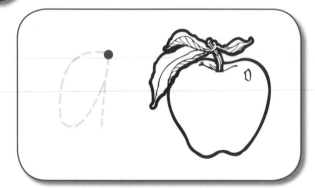

2 Match to a picture.

cat

bat

sat

mat

fat cat

I am Sam.